AF335365

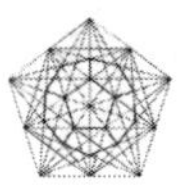

This volume of poetry is dedicated to

Sally, my sister, and David, her husband,
whose love and loyalty, care and wise counsel,
welcome, generosity and rich hospitality
enrich all our family life,

and to

Angharad,
their daughter, my niece and only god-daughter,
whose presence, personality and perceptions
enhance and encourage our daily lives.

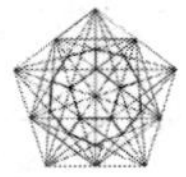

Andrew Francis at Avebury, Summer Solstice, 2011

EARTH AIR FIRE WATER

Poems by Andrew Francis

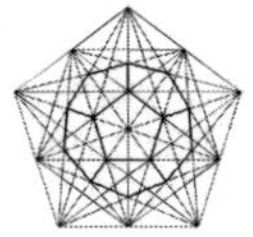

With an Introduction

by the author

THE KETTLE PRESS

Bristol 2016

First published in 2016 by
The Kettle Press, an imprint
of Imagier Publishing
Bristol BS35 3SY
United Kingdom
Email: ip@imagier.com
www.imagier.com

© Andrew Francis
The right of Andrew Francis to be identified as
the author of this work has been asserted by him in
accordance with the Copyright, Designs and Patents Act 1988

All rights reserved.
No part of this publication may be reproduced,
stored in or introduced into a retrieval system,
or transmitted in any form, or by any means, electronic,
mechanical, photocopying, recording or otherwise,
without the prior written permission of the publisher.
Reviewers may quote brief passages.

ISBN 13: 978-1-910216-13-2

Cover and text design by Allan Armstrong

The paper used in this publication is from a
sustainable source and is elemental chlorine free.

Printed and bound by Booksfactory.co.uk

CONTENTS

PREFACE

Kettle Press is an imprint of Imagier Publishing, dedicated to publishing contemporary 'spiritual' poetry originating in Wessex and the West Country.

At the Kettle Press we acknowledge that all poetry is an intimate expression of a poet's thoughts and reflections on a given subject. This is especially so with spiritual poetry, which has the power to express the most profound thoughts and convey complex feelings in ways that can, in an instant, move the reader or listener into another mode of discernment.

Once published, such intimate creations simultaneously become both personal and public. The private reader is invited to pause, take in each poem and reflect upon it. Publicly, the poems are available beyond the private moment, whether read from a public stage or discussed within a group. In either case engaging with spiritual poetry is not simply an intellectual or metaphysical exercise but a 'spiritual' experience reaching far beyond the mind into the heart and soul of the reader. It is for this purpose the Kettle Press came into being.

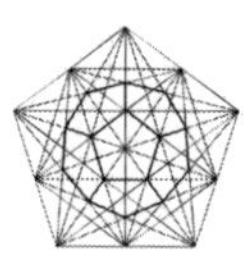

ACKNOWLEDGEMENTS

I am grateful to Rowan, one of my pagan acquaintances, for the nudge towards this book – and its title. I am also grateful to the many folk around, predominantly British, but some Irish and Manx, as well as mainland European for conversations, experiences or the discovery of 'place', which each in their turn must have led to a poem.

Decades ago, in our twenties, I remember that my sister, Sally, and I both coincidentally weekended together, at our parents' then home. We spent Saturday morning, coffee-mugs in hand, talking poetry. In her MA English and Philosophy studies, Sally could resolutely advocate the work of Sylvia Plath and I was arguing a counterpoint from Ted Hughes' work. We both understood the importance of 'place' and the role of elemental spirits in the writing of poetry. Amongst her overwhelming generosity, Sally still provides me with poetry that challenges – her recent Christmas gift included volumes from both Jo Shapcott and Kate Tempest. I thank my Creator daily for Sally and her family – hence this book's dedication.

I am grateful, too, to those many people (particularly in Cornwall, County Durham, Merseyside, Lancashire and Yorkshire) who, back in the day, produced poetry magazines on duplicators in back bedrooms or ran poetry evenings in pubs, colleges and clubs, giving my (and others') earlier work an airing. Our Wiltshire Stanza group, local poetry slams and recitals, have all further helped the genesis of this book.

My partner, Janice and her daughter Caroline, cope with my bits of paper, the scattered notebooks, chuntering of couplets and occasional delays to al fresco meals as I scribble down a few more lines, check a word or sketch a landscape.

Finally, I remain indebted to Allan Armstrong, the managing editor of Imagier, (but more like a brother than a distant publisher) who has published this volume under their Kettle Press (poetry) imprint. But also to you, the reader, for taking time to take this from the shelf...enjoy what you read! God bless you all.

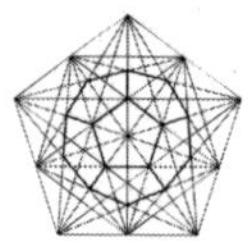

INTRODUCTION

Long before the age of Harry Potter caused many contemporary readers to talk about 'the philosopher's stone', it formed part of the thinking about the classical elements. That stone was allegedly able to turn dross into gold or dust into silver and the search for it, rivalled that for the Holy Grail. This stone was referred to in some of the best English poetry and Christian hymnody.

Those classical elements were earth, air, fire, water. They formed much of the basis of medieval English alchemy, although scholars now tend to agree that this in turn was drawn from Persian sources. Whatever of that particular truth, once humanity is awakened to the soul, it desires to learn not only of God but of the elemental origins of life. Hence earth, air, fire, water. In their various measures these take on aspects of the senses of cold, dry, heat, wet, helping us understand our very selves, the esoteric view of the universe and the 'tree of life'.

When considered in this broader way, we can further appreciate why those elements of earth, air, fire, water form part of Buddhist, Chinese, Egyptian, Japanese and Tibetan, as well as pagan European, thought forms and spirituality and influenced Greek Aristotelianism. In touching so many cultures and civilisations, earth,air, fire, water have both that elemental and global significance for much of the world's population, over the centuries. It was hardly surprising to me that the globally successful Florence and the Machine began their June 2015 headlining set at the Glastonbury Festival with her song 'What the water gave me' telling how this elemental spirit speaks into contemporary culture.

My personal journey and interest in earth, air, fire, water is increasingly revealed both in these poems and at the end of this slim volume. Not all of these poems may seem intensely religious or Christian but they are about the experience of 'being alive' and in touch with one's senses and the planet and people around us. These are things which give our earthly lives, both body and soul, their meaning and locus in 'the greater scheme of things'. That is the spiritual quest which all humanity desires...

We do this despite our imperfections. I am always consoled by the fact that Amish and Quaker folks deliberately have some planned inadequacy in their quilts because 'nothing is perfect'. When I played and sang more publicly, I was grateful of the audience's joyful, encouraging applause when one of us hit a wrong chord or sang 'a bum note'. I am grateful that folks still drink out of my (past) hand-thrown mugs despite each vessel's slight differences. I rejoice that I believe in a God of forgiveness, because my life is peppered with mistakes, inadequacies and imperfections.

Poetry is both personal and public. Although it is written privately and is intensely personal, it becomes public as soon as it is published, declaimed before any audience or even passed from the writer to a confidante. In revealing a writer's poem, its imperfections and inadequacies become apparent. Why did s/he not say this? Or use a different metre or more allusion or alliteration? The art of poetry is like a hand-thrown pot, a performed song, a hand-made quilt, a painting – it is the best it can be on the day when it is given over to others. It reveals the writer's search for meaning, their sense of the world around them and the people who help forge their human existence. Poetry thus exists, despite the imperfections and inadequacies of the poet – if not, I could not have let these fifty-three poems be published.

But in any poem becoming public, it has that sense of illumination. Not just of what the writer is seeking after but it also invites the reader to consider searching beyond the everyday encounter, whether it is with a pebble, a peacock, a preconception or another person. This is why poetry is elemental – because it invites us to wrestle with the mundane or special and to move to the meaning beyond the simply existential. None of us can live without earth, air, fire, water – nor the challenge of poetry to our soul. Our inter-reaction with them may leave us cold/analytical – dry/philosophical – heated/excited – wet/emotional. Poetry should provoke, illuminate and challenge. It should cause change In effect, poetry can become 'the philosopher's stone' if we can but let it, helping us move beyond the dross of much everyday thinking.

So I offer you some more of my poetry, which collectively has been gathered as *'Earth Air Fire Water'*. These fifty three pieces have come together over the past twenty years, knowing both recasting and revision, but offering insight into how the questions of the elemental world affect us now. Where do we choose to let our eye, mind and heart rest. One verse of a centuries-old famous poem known as *'The Elixir'* says this:

The man that looks on glass,
on it may stay his eye,
or if he pleaseth through it pass
and then the heaven espy.

These words by George Herbert (1593-1633), the priest and poet, became part of one of the standard and much-loved contributions of Christian hymnody. It concludes:

> This is the famous stone
> which turneth all to gold:
> for that which God doth touch and own
> cannot for less be told.

The concept that what we have to offer is of our best, and yet of the everyday substance of being, and the world, is vital. It is both elemental and life-giving in that what we bring becomes 'the philosopher's stone', not just questioning the world but seeing beyond the limitations of that which is purely physical, perfunctory and often imperfect.

AMDG
Summer solstice 2015   Andrew Francis

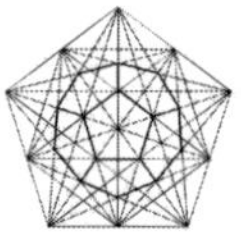

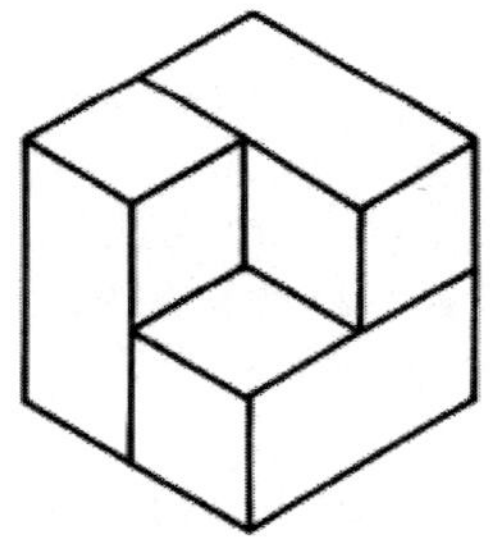

Earth

ALDERLEY EDGE

I came, looking for the weirdstone, not really for Brisinga men,
learning this mythical but real landscape as a child:
its mis-shapen trees, rock formations and steep drops.
Together with friends, we swung away across ravines and then
discovered hidden silver rivulets
          — teeming streams of nature wild,
building dens for the afternoon deep in a woodland copse.
The stories which Alan had garnered
          turned boys into warrior men
fighting battles against the forces unseen,
          our minds undefiled
by adult thought, human compromise, political sops.

I came, in need of a cool pint,
          after walking down from the Edge.
The Queen's Hotel beckoned
          but something stopped me instead,
for this was another world – false like childhood dreams.
Littered with its designer shops, and more, driving a wedge
between the footballers' wags, their beaus with their cars,
          all shiny and red,
and those who lived here long before
          fashion's designer teams.
Now the nouveau-riche perch in each restaurant's
          well-lit window ledge
needing to be seen, fawned over,
          more stars than thoughts in their styled heads.
Another fabricated world, more froth than real life means.

I came, to interview Wilfrid Garlick for the old BBC
      —he of *'The Parson Calls'*, now long since here retired,
taping his memories in a large curtained room.
Reminding me of John Evans' hermitage by the old oak tree;
Evans' scandal caught up with him,
      found dead, his reputation now mired
with ambiguities, thick as mud in the Edge's gloom.
Evans died at whose hand,
      Garlick in his chair but what death for you and me
unfolds as we still walk that Edge, in dawn,
      dusk , dark, feeling tired
awaiting that 'Boneland', a final chapter-sealing tomb ✋

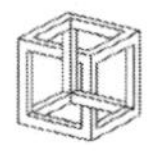

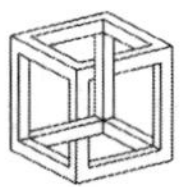

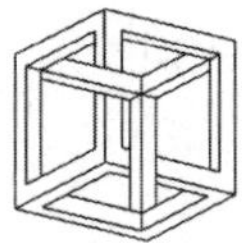

ALL THIS CAN BE YOURS...

'The meek shall inherit the earth'
but only when the rich and greedy have had their fill.
When their armies and henchmen have plundered,
      raped and killed
what will be left for the common man?
And who will save the violated woman...?
...when the dying ends and the war drums are stilled

'Blessèd are the poor in spirit'
yet the world leaders keep their pride and hangers-on,
as the children starve, droughts occur, disease gallops on.
What will then be left for those left without
and prophets who question, rage and doubt?
As the World Bank tempts with *'all this can be yours'*...

'Blessèd are the peacemakers'
but only when the arms dealers have all gone broke?
What price the world's momentum to accept that death
      and war are wrong?
What will be left of a scorched barren earth
then who will scratch our living or bring to birth
the future hopes of all...or terminal oblivion? ❧

AVALON

As the soul is lost in mystery
and the mist dims all that you can see,
the legend of the Tor remains,
heralding the connections with Arthur's might.
For now the growth of Arimathea's thorn
with its berry of red and whiteness of leaves,
tells the story of ancient Avalon.

When the mind is lost in history
and the monks die on the gallows tree,
the death of the Abbey's proclaimed,
foretelling the Protectorate's march into night.
Back then, it brought a renewed half-dawn
of pilgrims and saints and monastic hours,
risking the marsh to escape death's talon.

If the heart goes to Glastonbury
and it transforms into what you want it to be,
the high path song of the Tor's refrain,
beckons you on as day becomes night.
For you the mist fragments in the dawn,
town, travellers and song magically re-appear
as you become one with the heart of Avalon. ❧

BRADDA HEAD

High above Mannin's southern cliffs,
        Milner's tower focuses the eye,
where the wild Loghtan sheep skittle rocks
        arcing through the sky,
to fall or bounce off outcrops into the sea,
        without trace to die.

Over four hundred feet,
        separates the tower's height from the sea below,
as gulls and kittiwakes scream and wheel
        and attack the marauding crow,
as below the spume,
        scuba divers brave the crystal deep in hope.

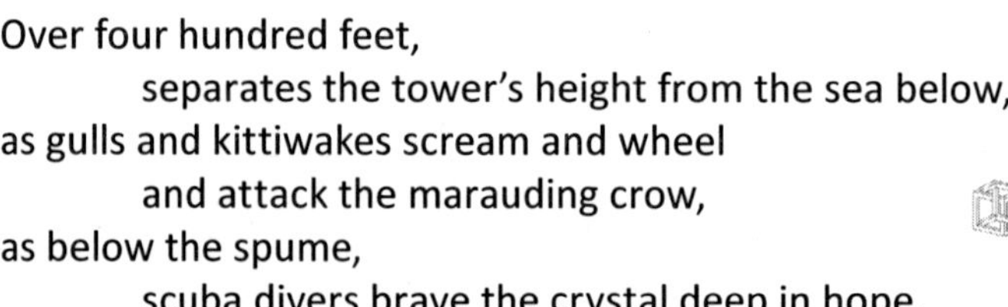

Nearly four hundred years before,
        men began to fish this coast,
gathering the great scallop harvest,
        in recent times to boast,
in pubs with tales of daring to achieve the most.

Yet nearly four thousand years before them,
        the cliffs were dug out by men,
creating shafts to mine copper
        — back in the Bronze Age, then.
Now those borings give shelter to artists,
        mining paint, ink and pen.

We struggle to climb from Port Erin to Bradda Head,
past the workings of the past
    and the workings of the dead,
to lounge in heather as the seabirds wheel
    and crow above our heads. ❧

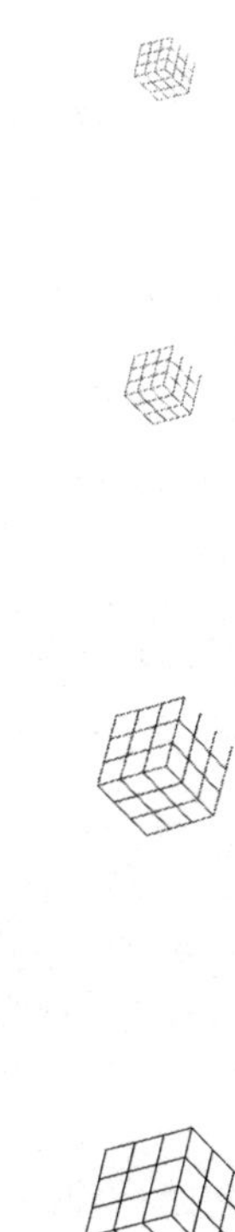

GOOD EARTH

It was rich and black, crumbling between my fingers,
the ground itself worked by my father's hard labour,
producing our food – season upon season.
His allotment, and that of our neighbour
growing memories too that linger.

It was dark and red, the earth of the Charente's hills,
the ground worked, generation upon generation
producing plenty, by hand, by horse, by tractor.
This land of soil, land of toil, soul of a nation
invades my heart, from summer's heat to winter's chill.

It was light and fawn, sandy loam of the Western Isles,
substrate for a sabbatical summer's crop
the ground planked round in raised beds.
Beans blown away, but carrots, radishes and lettuce
grew well enough, with tastes to make guests smile.

Then I moved to a plot of Wiltshire's boulder clay
rueing my misfortune as it bent my fork's tines
and puddled my land even in the summer's rains.
Letting the old boys help my garden skills refine
as I wished and longed for before, and a brighter day.

How I longed for that long Pennine sloping strip,
with its well-drained and fertile peaty loam,
where my beans stood tall and spuds were blight free.
Incredible, edible — the place I call home
as north calls me back and not just for a trip.

It was bright and red, that café on the street corner,
in politics, chat, home-made food and books,
part of an old church, now called 'The Good Earth'.
Like the town, it was good value, not famed for its looks,
but with a smile and a hope to outlive any mourner. ✑

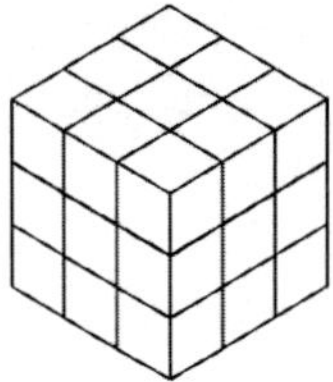

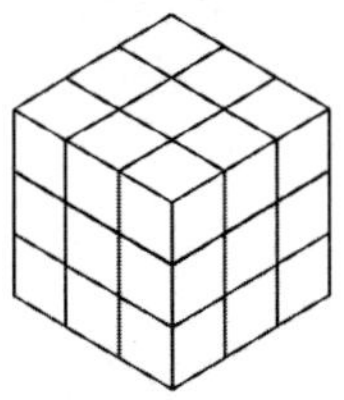

HEFTED

We did as instructed, "Leave the Midlands office by noon",
driving hard northwards up the motorway, turning inland.
The directions were good – I never expected they would not be
as road turned to lane, gated onto fellward track,
but there was their home, lights burning against dusk's gloom.

We embraced as old friends, "It's that long since your wedding?",
arriving hungry, we sat down to eat, laugh and chatter.
Pete's instructions were clear, by torch we checked house-cows,
        weaners and geese,
bedding them down, against weather in byre and shed,
melded into the hill like any Scots steading.

We breakfasted well, the sheep noisily declared this day,
Karen opened the gate and they skittered up the track.
It was hard graft after the third gate, as the herd led the way up
onto the open fell, mile after mile, we walked
until the herd scattered, knowing there they stay.

We left them high-on-the-moor,
        hefted into this - their landscape,
Walking back down, we diverted to the pub on the road.
The pints were well-earned, the bar meals were good
        as the place filled
with walkers, twitchers and farmers at their days' end,
all living their dreams, with no want of escape.

When Pete left the office, hard to believe, we were bereft,
our city boy joker decamped to join his shepherdess.
As he and I shot marauding rabbits in their veg patch
I knew he had changed into a north countryman,
grafted in like the sheep and the farm – hefted. 

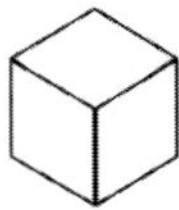

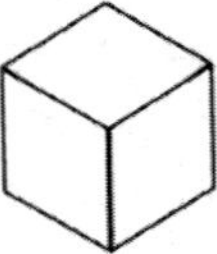

LEY LINES

Cartographer, mathematician, philosopher
Gerardus Mercator divided up our world,
inventing the future as he projected the world's future.

Historian, New-Age journeyman, philosopher
    John Michell strode from Avalon to Atlantis
        — a whole new world of dreams, visions
            projecting the world's past rule.

        And there is me, listening
        to the beat of a different drum,
        with wonder at raindrops glistening,
        and joy in a new loaf's crumb,
        or dismay at a child's christening.

        Housing London's Free School,
    becoming a sacred geometrician,
  John Michell moved from cigarette to desk to this
reflection: writer, campaigner, life's overseer.

Was it such an odd-shaped map, that projected nations' lines,
or perhaps confused minds preferring tradition
in life, on paper before the dreamers rethought earth. ❧

SNAEFELL

The tram ratchets its way like an electric caterpillar,
all the way up, close by the Laxey wheel.
Enviously watching, "Walking up's a killer"
exclaimed my fellow hiker, hungry for his next meal.

Arriving at the top, we could see for miles
       on this clear day:
could we reach and touch the Mull of Galloway?
Or think that Scafell Pike was only a fell or two away,
and that Snowdon's peak, a journey for another day?
Those Mountains of Mourne invite further holiday.
Yet in silence and wisps of cloudy grey,
we stood, reflecting that soon we would
       be on our downward way...

The tram rattled its way down whence it had come
       hours before
as we sat, shaken by the rails and wheels.
Fortified by a pint or two, we walked down to
       Douglas shore,
where we each ate double chips and fish
       as evening meals.

In that week, as we journeyed around
       the kingdom of Mann,
we were watched over by Snaefell's mount.
From Peel to Ramsey, Castletown to Curraghs,
       we would plan
to look up, knowing the mountain's eye
       kept watching beyond count. ❧

SPEM IN ALIUM

Creator caeli et terrae,
I can call out to no other
as I look at the work of your hands and mind
whether in metaphor or the dust that prefigured it all.
In the world all around — in all that I find,
in the life and face of each sister and brother:
Creator caeli et terrae.

Creator caeli et terrae,
I want my voice to sing in praise,
as I realise this world full of blessing,
Whether alone on the hill, small chapel or cathedral,
you draw from my lips words of faith confessing
amidst hours of doubt as well as glorious days:
Creator caeli et terrae.

Creator caeli et terrae
I know my need for you to bless
as I eat the harvest of earth, tree and field.
Whether alone, with my family or the community's hall,
all your gifts set around – our lives now to yield,
to your service, your call as we pledge of our best:
Creator caeli et terrae. ❧

NOTE: This poem was written after a winter picnic on a Cotswold ridge whilst iPod-listening to Thomas Tallis' meisterwerk *Spem in Alium*; the very translation of its title [Latin: hope in any other] being rejected in the glory of this 40 voice motet, affirming the Creator of heaven and earth.

STAFFA

Climb the steep steps beyond the smell of diesel
or skirt the basalt cliff to Fingal's cave,
humming the strains of Mendelssohn
as the tidal torrents drown one's own echoes away
then we wait alone before going back to the top.

Beneath swoops and cries of ocean-blown petrels,
the spume of bad weather rolls in like a single wave
— drumming of rain, an endless song,
then in a trice, the dark clouds are banished and away
whilst we wait as the sun warms us up.

Lying in low gorse, speckled with teasel,
the sights, smells and sounds, our senses enslave
— comes in the smack's bell to call our way home,
with thoughts to cherish, memories to save,
tearing our eyes from those of beach-bound seal pups. &

TERRA INCOGNITA

She used to be my neighbour, whom my kids called Auntie Joan;
she babysat for us and other neighbours, without fail.
Then she began to forget her grandchildren's names,
or to look at her kitchen calendar to post their cards
or to take her shopping list or remember her women's meeting.
One day, a kind policewoman brought her home,
Joan had forgotten to get off the train for the market
to find herself lost, three stops down the line.
We talked as fear clouded her journey to that twilight world,
between knowing and the unknowing,
fearful of the day that would come
fearful for the time when all memory was gone.
A fear known yet unknown
terror incognito.

Now she sits there vacantly as nurses say "Come on, Joan",
confined in a locked home, cared-for, secure as in a jail.
Her divorced son visits each week, as his work permits,
travelling across towns and cities in the north-west,
when no question makes any sense, except
       "What are you eating?"
Joan's daughter, 'down under', can't afford the flight
before her mother threw away the photo album, full of strangers,
her memories lost, now and for all time.
I listened to her son as he explored that twilight world,
between knowing and unknowing,
frightened of what his Mum had become,
frightened of the place with all remembrance gone.

A land known yet unknown
terra incognita.

The day came, an empty chair, no-one saying "Come on Joan",
her mind already gone had waited long enough
          for the rest to fail.
Her daughter phoned, saying that she would not be coming
"As her Mum had really died long ago and this was just goodbye",
so I stood with her son and his daughter at that service fleeting.
Joan's son and I cleared her house at week-ends,
tidying the garden and throwing away her final mementos,
her living expunged with an estate agent's sign.
I listened to myself as I feared that twilight world,
between knowing and unknowing,
frightened that that place might beckon me "Come!",
fearful of that place where all becomes none.
A land known yet unknown..... ๛

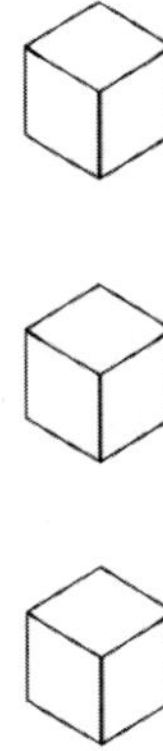

THE PEAK

The Peak

The Peak,
gritstone in the north.
A landscape that is foreign to my sight,
scudding clouds on a summer's day,
yet dark and foreboding in the cold light of dawn,
but the raptors, beyond recognisable sight,
hover and wait
for the sudden, darting movement of their next prey,
as the land is still in this place called
the Peak — with its' Dark Peak in the north.

Yet in its midst, the mile-upon-mile-upon mile
of peat moorland,
beloved of my grammar school's camp.
A field by Edale, sheltered in the valley,
dotted with bell-tents — white against the lush green of meadow,
like some anglicised Native American tipi gathering.
Mam Nick, Mam Tor, Ringing Roger:
we sat on their viewpoints, eating sardine sandwiches,
whilst the drone of schoolmasters competed with spring bees,
as we decided who would end up in the bog that afternoon.

[pause]

The Peak,
limestone in the south.
A landscape that grew common in my mind's eye,

drizzling rain on a walker's day,
yet dark and foreboding in the cold light of dawn,
but the field birds, invisible to our sight,
offer distinct calls
       — wind-borne, trilling so turning our ears to their sound,
as the land remains still in this place called
the Peak — with its' White Peak in the south.
[pause]

The Peak. ✎

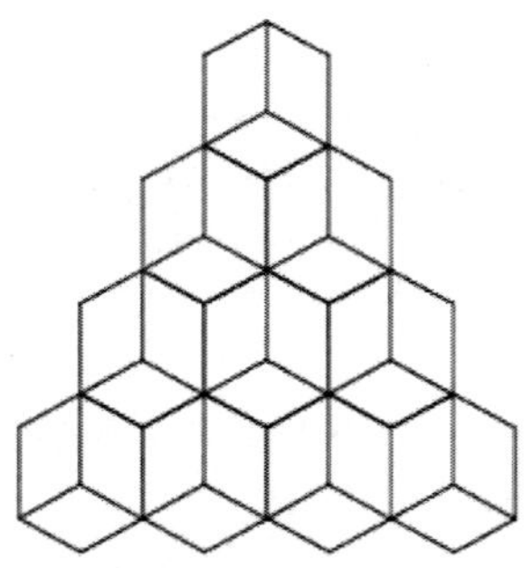

WATER MEADOWS

The river lulls and meanders its course.
Champing cattle, tails swishing, knee-deep
in its midstream, minnows at their feet conspire.
Here, I could waste many days without remorse,
just watching, wine glass in hand, for summer's sleep
or sketch away until the colours expire.
Here, teenage fumblings gave way to intercourse,
hid in mown grass, shovelled into a heap,
as the flow edged towards Salisbury's spire.

Memories crowd, my eyes entranced
towards shimmering green of willows' weep
as words of Brooke and Grantchester's muse inspire.
There I swam naked past a woman on her horse,
just watching, reins loose in hand, riverbank steep,
mutually pondering what might transpire:
there, exchanged greetings was the sum of our discourse.
Cambridge days drowned by the harvester's reap
as its noise edged through the meadows of the shire. ❧

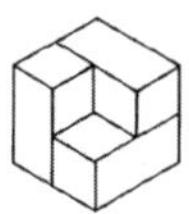

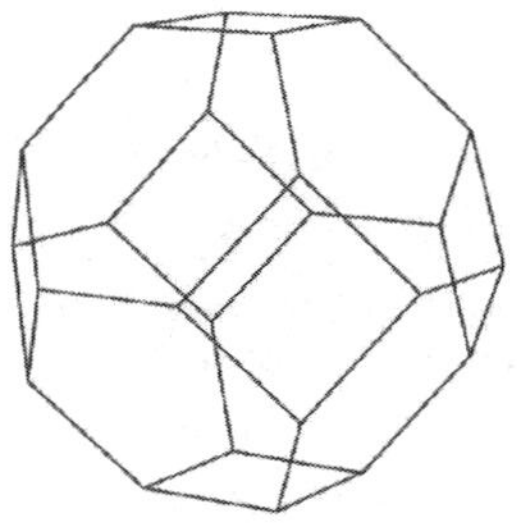

Air

AIRWAVES

The big, brown, Bakelite, Bush radio
stood on my grandparents' dresser,
booming out from the BBC
the best that the Light and Third could offer.
It was the audio wallpaper to our family life,
turned down or off when visitors came.
It was the fixture that brought us Big Ben,
New Years and all the world's news.

The big, brown, Bakelite, Bush radio
moved to my grandparents' last home,
standing on the phone-stand
next to my Grandpa's huge, leather chair.
Now the cat could sit on top, getting warmth from the valves
unless bowls of proving dough were there first.
This new family room had the same sound,
same broadcast voices, some renowned.

The bright, yellow, transistor radio
replaced my school-made cat's whisker,
listening late at night
to the pirates, London and Caroline.
Then the first day of Radio One, music from the Move,
on the move, all day — I was battery-powered.
Far more than pick of the pops, there's John Peel,
Rosko, new names as the old stars just soured.

The silver sheen of my new system,
hi-fi! — boxes, tuner, wires, speakers,
changed the way music and news arrived
in my young, free and single, flat-share days.
Now everything is in glorious stereo
concerts from the Proms, Pink Floyd, progressive rock.
Jazz on Three, Folk on Two, now news on Four,
pre-tuned stations arriving on the clock.

The solid, reliable Roberts radio
moved the airwaves around in line with my life,
from the kitchen window-ledge
to the studio with its wheel and easel.
Now anything is industrially mono,
Classic FM as the clay's in my hands,
Jazz FM used to help me to paint,
transporting my life to distant lands.

The house is now littered with digital boxes,
with their faux wood and Art Deco finishes,
and more digital stations than there is time
to even discover or listen.
But *Today* hardly seems to change, as
the bad news, our minds enslave.
Almost unable to tune away from
that which still comes from those airwaves. ❧

August 6

Was it just another August day
when the world lost its way
as a US priest blessed the Enola Gay?
Deadly payload aboard and flight check done,
the crew hand-picked for this mission,
the plane took off on its historic run.

Something's in the air?

The Japanese nuns began to pray
in that cathedral's day
not knowing their fate sealed on maps far away.
Hiroshima went about its routine,
unaware, beyond clouds, unseen
to the eye, death was coming: crude and mean.

Fire in the sky

So, how can the Church begin to pray
"Forgive our sins this day",
yet bless the bomb and target their nuns that day?
No longer can warfare be declared as just
when land is scorched, with burning lust
as people and buildings are fried to dust

Something in the air...

Today, we still pay that dust-cloud's price
of hate, greed, human vice,
threatening our planet like a roll of dice.
As August sixth's cancers still burn away
in Japanese bodies to this day,
inviting us to stop: change our warring way. ❧

FRAGRANT LIGHT

The glass orb swirls from the window's breeze,
its suspending ribbon masked by sunlight's glare.
That loved gift from my sister
refracts the brightness
and scents the summer's air.

Its indigo-blue daubs and yellow-ochre stripes
striate patterns across the wooden floor.
The colours dance their slow waltz,
tracing gliding steps
all unique, without encore.

The teardrop within hides its secret —
fragrant oil dropped in water, warmed by orb-held air.
That fragrance weaves within the unseen breeze
as sure as warp and weft
as the day decides what to wear... ❧

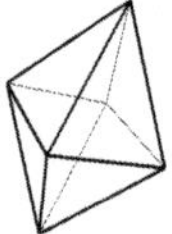

HEAVEN SCENT

I love the smell of your garden's arbour at evening,
that industrially trellised pergola full of climbing roses,
forming both veranda and terrace to your summerhouse,
as the perfume of summer's bloom entrances our noses.
We adjourn to its' evening shade with bottle and glass,
after watering the plants from butts and hoses;
one remembers the moment, never wanting it to pass.
Heaven's scent.

The ruby richness of the red wine,
the lemony smoothness of the *Pilgrim* rose,
the taste of salt from the sea-borne breeze...
...and then there is you
heaven sent.

I love the way that we can sit on that arbour bench,
as you tilt your tired head to rest on my shoulder
as the sun slides away, and the light dies into night,
the bats and fireflies distract as the dusk gets colder.
I smell your soap and the evening in your hair,
worrying in case my senses diminish as I grow older;
one remembers this moment, always wanting to be there.
Heaven sent. ❧

INCENSE

Within whitewashed walls, candles
warm stone chill that disarms:
the cassocked monk sells us
incense to burn with our prayers
beneath the blue domes.
Santorini's olive grove balm
refreshes tired city bodies.

Contrast English cathedrals'
sense of something's lost balm:
the prayer and holiness,
incense, silence, candles
corralled in side chapels.
God is distant — archaic as psalms,
incensing our minds in their loss.

Santiago's cathedral,
echoes with chanting psalm:
the swinging thurible's
incense fills the huge space
above our heads.
Journey's end — a sense of calm,
celebrating our pilgrimage.

In the prior's book-lined study,
there's that innate sense of calm:
the singing is distant
yet incense fills the air,
inspiring talk.
Holy time — its peace disarms,
restoring that in which we believe. ❧

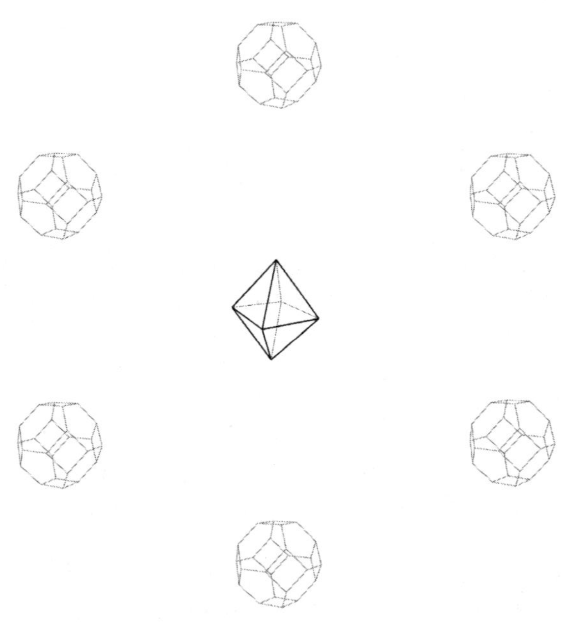

MEVAGISSEY

The light seeped then flooded through the thin linen curtains
      sea-bleached,
drawing them back, I opened windows for July's warmth
      to reach in.

We lay, with our morning tea, drinking the day ahead into life
thinking of plans, we started to smile as the hours could stretch
      and fly before us.

Breakfasted, we wandered to the familiar baker, chatting
      on our way
as seagulls chorused high above our heads as others
      bade us 'good day'.

Picnic made, wine on ice, we stepped out along the coastal path
to that secret beach, where we swam, slept, read the papers,
      expressed our wrath.

As we returned, the tide was out, exposing all to the
      brackish smell;
we sat with our wine, in the tiny courtyard, as halyards
      rang their evening bell.

The dabs, bread and camembert all waited their turn on the grill,
as we ate and watched the sun sink again beyond
      that distant hill.

Throwing on layers, we talked as the stars turned on their lights
whilst below at harbourside, the crowds dispersed
      into the night. ❧

MIGRATION

From lone to skein into flight,
the migration began.
Wind forming water into wave
lapping hard to spruce-lined shore.
The same strong currents lifting
wings into powerful beating.
Air to rise, geese into sky,
knowing winter is knocking at the door.

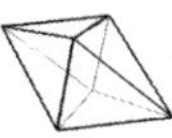

From nest to egg into brood,
the young goslings began.
Risk causing venture, sink or swim,
driving them into first dive.
Marauding pike — still a threat
spoiling life in the summer sun.
Now! For change, wing into sky
testing the ability to survive.

From slung to cocked to shoulder,
the hunters' rifles held.
Need pushing hunger into chase
forcing men to snow-dazed shoot.
Dogs retrieving, drop the 'kill',
necks snapped, gutting, long-quill plucking.
Heat and grease, bird into pie
giving meat for the table, bread, bean and root.

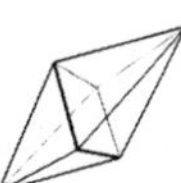

From shot to sound to death
puncturing the whole skein
Goose falling earthward into reeds,
breaks pattern of southbound flight.
Old patterns woven each fall
of leaves, as with beat of wings,
autumn comes — migration now
for thousands more as sure as day turns to night. ❧

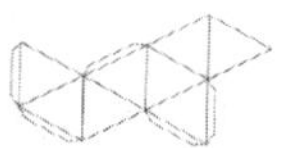

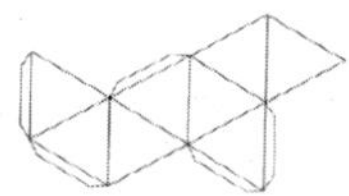

Raw

The air was raw.
"Raw this morning" greeted the farmer
to the cowhand, whistling the dog
herding the cows through the gate
towards the milking shed.

The wind was raw
piercing like arrowheads through armour
unseen, silent as falling fog
gusting the flames back to grate
making our limbs feel dead.

Dawn still felt raw,
as the wind dropped, feeling much calmer.
Trudging through the crisp frozen bog
finding lambs dead to their fate
feasting crows now well-fed.

Noon – not so raw,
mist wrapped the day, nothing to harm there,
journeying back, armfuls of logs
evening's warmth to await
cold bones ready for bed.

Dusk came in raw
"Raw again now" noted the farmer
to the cowhand, whistling the dog
herding the cows through the gate
into the milking shed. ❧

SLIMBRIDGE

Wing-beats heard, then dark against the sky, they came
in skeins, in pairs, solo, the landing splash, the avian scrum.

Greylag	Whitefront	Pinkfoot
Divers	Moorhen	Coot
Bewick's	Whooper	Mute

Marsh-ward bound, dressed green to match the brush, we walk
ten by fifties to hand, hushed excitement, so little talk.

Rushy hide	Rushy pen
Tropical House	Zeiss Hide
Duck decoy	Swan Pond
Sloane Tower	Peng Observatory

Nature rich, variety exposed, feathers
coloured or dulled, beauty iridescent, in all weathers

Andean	Caribbean	James
Common	Demoiselle	Cranes
Saltmarsh	Wetland	Cockaigne

Ducks, more ducks, eider, mallard, teal, beyond
our counting, we leave, sadly wondering when we can next
abscond...

The starling mass wheels, like our thoughts, into air
        —yet another world beyond?

'STARLESS AND BIBLE-BLACK'

The sky was dark, beyond belief:
its evening lights, shrouded in cloud,
as we turned out from Birmingham's town hall,
our ears still ringing from the Crimson ride
into mountain halls and worlds beyond our thought.
A great-coated army of long-haired young men
dissipating into the starless night,
with pretentious talk about new albums bought,
kebabs to hand, late-night buses boarded.
Now King Crimsonned, new memories hoarded.
starless but never Bible-black!

The sleep was full, bringing relief,
its dark stupor reining in pain.
As he turned away from another concert hall,
their ears still ringing from the Thomas' verse
of Llaregub and wrestled nights of thought.
A fur-coated army of hair-permed women,
over-inflated talk by critics and noisome men,
"It's nineteen fifty-three".
No canting priest then? Just ever more whisky,
Dylan was always Bible-black.

The shed still stands — a homage to grief;
its river-view framing his gain,
as we turned up to where he began it all.
Our ears still ringing with remembered lines
from books of prose and verse plucked from nought.
A well-coated army of well-prepared fans,
hyper-inflated talk silenced by moment and place
in this village of Laugharne.
Death made him legend, almost safe from harm:
we are not starless but still Bible-black. ❧

THE SKY AT NIGHT

(for Patrick)

Sometimes I wonder at the sky at night
wishing the clouds would soon disappear
unclothing the stars
letting my eyes roam into depths of space

Sometimes I learned about the sky at night
discovering more as things became clear
just watching the stars
letting my mind travel to that unknown place

But now, I want to know more that sky at night
wanting to find worlds beyond our fear
still watching those stars
realising that I'm less than a point on the galaxy's face

Often I heard him say of the sky at night
"Don't strain, patience, let them just appear"
revealing new stars
belittling our self-made importance as the human race ❧

SUNDOWN

With the shadow of Cader far to the north,
we sat on the salt-bleached garden sleepers,
Aberporth's sheltered bays, three streets below,
as the cries of evening gulls died away,
seeking their roosts in the rocks and town's chimney-crags.
The day was nearly spent
as the sun's rays dipped their toes into the far horizon.

The idle bark of a beach-walked dog,
the distant laugh of a girl on the breeze,
the thrum of a summer tractor wending home:
the sounds of evening were coming home to roost, too.

It was nearly sundown.
We sat – feeling evening's warmth ebbing away
as the red wine warmed in our glass
contrasting with the cool of the spent day.
Reflecting on that day, our day well-spent,
as sleep beckoned us back inside,
the sun was now reflected on the far tide
which glistened silver horizon-wide.

The salt of sea-spray had climbed the headland,
the scent of dog-roses from the hedge at our backs,
all mixed with the citronella from a table candle:
the aroma of evening coming to the fore...

Sundown is now,
as we listen to the sizzling of the orb
as it dies orange into the sea,
painting the sky in myriad streaks.
The far headland cliffs glow with the dying of the light
as distant hills are ribboned with gold to the stars.
Day is done — the sun is gone and night has come. ৯

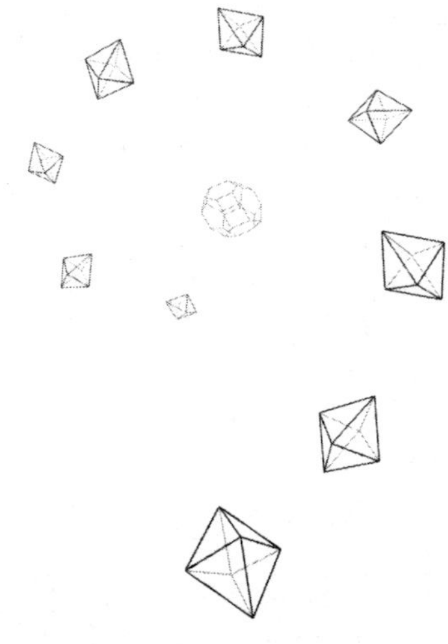

WEIHNACHTSMARKT

It was going to be a long weekend.
The Friday evening coach pick-up,
after a snatched fish and chips supper on the bus
        home from work.
The midnight Eurostar blurred its way to France,
our eyes closing, minds dulling as if in a trance,
then sleep stole our time as the coach drove
        through night's mirk.

It was going to be a long morning.
The autobahn's breakfast-time fry-up
weighed heavy on the stomach as the antacids did their work.
We checked in to our edge-of-town hotel,
a shower, a nap, with no real time to tell
then we were dropped off by carollers outside
        the town-centre kirk.

It was going to be a long evening.
The Christmas list of presents to buy up
as we hustled around the stalls, changing ideas for things
        that would work.
The starlings roosted - on came the Christmas lights
beading the stalls and buildings into rainbow sights,
but with it came evening rain, cobblestones to glisten yet
        no shelter in which to lurk.

It proved to be a very long night,
before our coach's one a.m. pick-up
of bag-laden, beer-filled tourists, würst for wear outside
    the Old Kirk.
Steins had been filled and drunk, roast pork eaten,
the man in the dancing bear costume had been beaten
around the Old Square and Christmas stalls,
    all singing along which no-one shirked.

It proved to be a longer day
with our ten a.m. German brunch,
before boarding our coach for miles of road, short stops,
    the Chunnel with its duty-free perk.
The English night was already upon us at Folkestone,
more miles of foggy motorway, our coach seemed alone
journeying home and into that Sunday night
    — the usual Weihnachtsmarkt visit's quirk. ✌

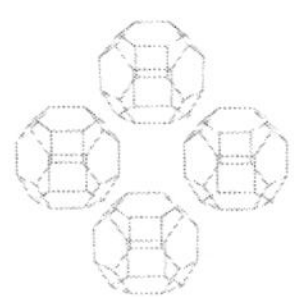

Fire

AWEN - AMEN

Awen — an old Cornish word,
yet part of my daily round,
meaning 'inspiration'
it is a fire burning deep from within the soul.
Flowing as three elements, splendid,
as spirit from the cauldron that is god of all.
Yet it marks the rays of brightness streaming,
like a tripod of ash staves
from three points of time as triads of sunrise.
The fire of light burns as time in the universe.
Awen — the understanding of truth,
Awen — the maintaining of truth.
Awen — the love of truth

One
becomes
Three
as the
Three
becomes
One.

Amen — an old Hebrew word,
yet part of my daily round,
meaning 'affirmation'
it is acclaim sung from deep within the soul.
Flowing as three known facets, triune,
as expressed from origins that is god in all.

Yet it marks the ways of sightless believing,
for hopeful crowds of faith's slaves
with three revelations point to Sonrise.
The fire of faith burns as time in the universe.
Amen — the understanding of truth,
Amen — the maintaining of truth,
Amen — the love of truth. ❧

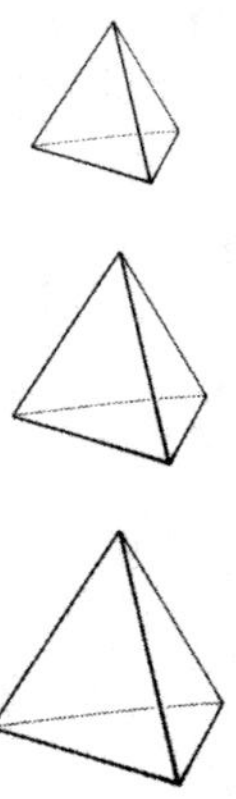

BLUE HAZE

Stuart was meant to take me to the Saturday matinee,
but he spent the time adoring the usherette.
A teenage queen earning her Saturday wage,
who piled up her tresses like Rita Hayworth,
and languidly stood, smoking her cigarette.
Slowly, so slowly
she blew smoke rings,
which widened as blue haze above wee children's heads,
as Stuart's eyes widened with lust
and the gunsmoke cleared to reveal the B-western's dead.

Grandpa always used to take us to Ladypool Road park,
where he bided time watching us play on the swings.
An upright man yearning for rich family life,
who stood, his pipe full of tobacco,
which he purposefully lit with one match.
Coldly, so coldly,
he puffed away
as we winter-walked back up the hill for bath and high tea,
then our eyes widened with joy,
as tar bubbled and blue haze clouded our evening story. ໑

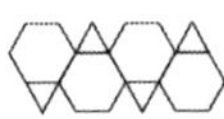

EMBERS

Tom and I used to sit in his terraced home, reminiscing
of his days, down the pit, as his cheap free coal
      spat back, hissing.

Since Elsie died, he had only kept the two fireside chairs;
 he sat with his back to the window to remain unawares.

He sat mainly silent, watching the flames erupt and die,
thinking hard, not even understanding how to ask 'why?'

We would talk, of the pithead bell or buttons-down-the-back,
his coal-dusted allotment, or walking the cliff-top track.

Glancing from Elsie's photo on the mantel down to dying embers,
his love, his life, the pit — are all that he remembers. ❧

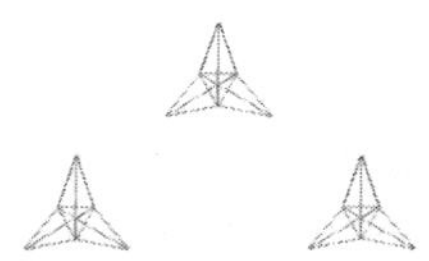

FIREFLIES

It quickly became part of our summer camp ritual,
that twice each week,
we would have a sundown camp-fire on the beach.
During the day, we would collect up a stash of sticks
between the swimming, sunning and volleyball matches.
We had our regular spot,
arriving with children, dogs, hangers-on and lunch,
used enough that we had a created a rock-lined firepit,
high above the tide line in the fine dry sand.
Those with children arrived early enough
to ensure that we built up camp over the day,
collecting up driftwood for that evening's stay.

It quickly became part of that summer camp ritual
that two singletons would stay,
guarding our cliff-sheltered sun-trap down at the beach.
After the day, we collected up tired children
making our way back across the heath, to the tents.
We had our camp-site routine,
showering the youngsters and giving them their tea,
sharing the chores, to create a clan-like life together,
below the dusk, children snuggled into their dreams.
Three used to stay in the camp on those nights
as others carried the grills and coolboxes back to the beach.
The fire was lit, we watched the food cook, faces aglow.

It quickly became part of that evening fire ritual,
to drink chilled white wine,
whilst sharing our evening meal on those nights at the beach.
After the food, we gathered up our lives with song
between the moments of talk, laughter and silence
We had our usual routine,
that on moonlit nights we would skinny-dip in the sea,
watching the fireflies dance and storm at the shoreline,
Below the moon, we dived and swirled 'til the tide warmed.
Then shivering with cold, run back and put wood on the fire,
bodies aglow and bobbling as we towelled ourselves dry
        then warm
before in the stillness, following the fireflies back to our tents. ❧

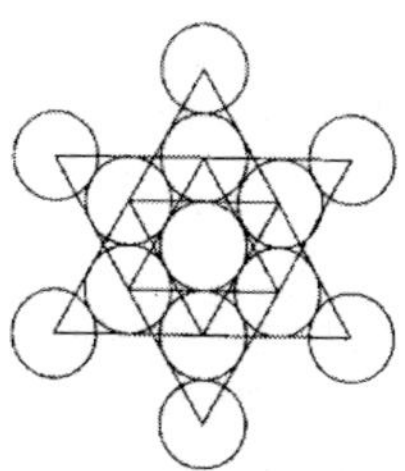

INCENDIUM AMORIS

It was in the dim-lit recesses of that dust-bound library…

I read of that Piers Plowman,
my mind taking unbridled step after another,
just one passus then another in alliterative tone.
Four visions unfolding,
in twenty progressing parts,
as our minds wrestled with Middle English
and the theories of Skeat.

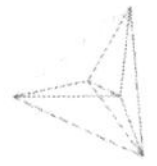

I knew of that Julian of Norwich
my heart taking unfettered leaps in meditation,
just one pause to reflect on another's revelations.
Those visions unfolding
in the cell above St. Julian's
as our minds wrestled with Warrack's new text,
knowing that all shall be well.

I saw the soul of Richard Rolle,
my love for God prised open by his discerned words
without source other than his text in a spiritual tome.
Four visions unfolding,
through that open door, then searing heat
that eternal song and divine sweetness, expressed in Latin
as Watson tried to change our thinking.

>   …our eyes raised in wonder
>   towards each other
>   above the ancient illuminated texts.

What of that man known as Meister Eckhart?
Whose theology work embraced a world of change,
shaping souls for centuries yet to come?
His vision unfolding
afresh by theosophist, modernists,
Buddhists in today's voices, rather than High German,
and by New Age market stall traders.

What of those folk called Rhineland Mystics,
from Tauler and Suso, Mechtild of Magdeburg
Nicholas Cusa, and aunt and niece nuns Ebner.
Their visions unfolding
from Strasbourg's free thinking and prayer
through nights "zum das fliessende Licht der Gottheit",
we became Gottfreunde zusammen.

What of that holy woman named Hildegard?
whose life was enclosed at the age of eight,
with a sister nun recorded as Jutta.
Her visions unfolding,
in liturgical song and three tomes of God-talk
Speaking to the masses, deep in their vernacular
and now unto us in the shades of our brave new world.

    ...our lips pursed in delight
    humming the Psalter
    above the ancient illuminated texts. ❧

IRIDESCENCE

We sat, drinking wine, in that Shetland courtyard
further north than if in Stockholm.
We were in the land of 'simmer dim',
the gloaming as those far in the south called it.
Not really night, so little dawn catches one off-guard.

We sat, sky watching, through the long bright night
as clouds ribboned high above us
in streams of green, neon blue, orange,
yellow, salmon-pink and red till horizon's end.
setting our faces aglow, forgetting how late the night.

We watched, minds agog, humming Renaissance:
the Northern Lights were in our eyes.
Even more food could not distract us,
nor Annie Haslam's beauty compare to the fire above
as the sky was inflamed by nature's iridescence. ❧

LE GREL

Father Neil used to preside at an old stone altar,
in a battered, rundown Salford church.
This barn of a place, with more pigeons than people
faithfully saying their prayers and the rubric's rites.
Cars were vandalised, the vicarage was burgled.
As a priest, he was abused and beaten-up,
the bishop and archdeacon left him in the lurch
caught between serving those he loved and just surviving.
Increasingly sad and fearful,
there was a choice to be made
and that Salford parish rang its last bell.

Maître Neil now presides over a hot charcoal grill,
in a sun-drenched and blessed Dordogne courtyard.
An old barn at its side, with its doves and people,
unfaithfully playing their stares on summer nights.
Few were scandalised, as the campsite soon encircled.
As mein host, he was respected and soon up-beat,
as tourists came, choosing pork, chicken or beef à la carte,
with as much white or red wine, so business was thriving.
Increasingly glad and beerful,
the right choice had been made
to step into France and new life at 'Le Grel' ❧

LIFE IN SLOW-BURN

With just two bob for the meter,
we would snuggle down in your bedsit.
As the gas fire struggled into flame,
we would play the music of those student days
on our precious guitars or battered hifi.

With new jobs, and a plug-in heater,
we would struggle in our new bedsit,
as we juggled adult lives into shape.
We would stay out late, watching plays
and economise eating baked beans and cheap pies.

Cooker hobs, carpets, a mixer-beater –
all part of our suburban subset.
Mortgaged, family life is the claim,
as shattered, we drop off at the end of days,
the smiling windows betray our love's lies.

Tearful sobs, regrets, life is no neater
after "that affair" lost our love-nest.
Centrally-heated wasted lives maimed
by our failures, and the parting of ways,
living alone just waiting until one of us dies. ❧

MIDSUMMER FEAST

Gypsy caravans had encircled the dell,
these hired vardas and wagons live in the memory well.
When we started, we were hardly wranglers
as it took over an hour to catch and rein-up the
      morning's horse.
So when we stopped for the day by some fast-flowing stream,
our lack of skill showed as we pretended to be anglers.
Four couples of friends, with their kids and their dogs,
learning the tricks of the road with each new day's course,
travelling at horse-walk, causing car drivers to fume
      and to steam.
Mid-fortnight, we Sunday stopped, with tents for two nights,
giving the horses a break and parents chance for love,
      hid in the gorse.
Each day, someone cycled to the shops
buying wine, bread, papers and meat
before hanging the bike on its hook on a van-back.
Eggs, fruit and veg were bought at the roadside
whilst cottagers petted the horses and our children told tales
of life "on the road, since we had left Wales".
On our last Thursday, with only five miles back to the cars,
we pitched up in a field by a sweeping bend of the Wye,
pitching the children's tents as the caravans encircled the dell.
We tethered the horses, lay in a sun which no memory mars,
we shopped in the village, bought food for a feast,
drank beer in the day and wined into the night,
when the camp-fire provided heat in the moonlight,
trout on the grill, salads in a dish, beef-stew in the pot,
      - hardly complaining, we ate and drank the lot. ✎

PALETTE

If I had painted like John Bratby or Mondrian or even
      old Bonnard,
I would have had a palette full of colour,
so bright, so vivid that it would make your eyes ache.
With one's mind on fire and nothing duller,
even my white would be titanium and not that of plain flake.

I never could paint like Corot, Whistler, Monet, Renoir or Pissarro,
however much my head was full of their scenes
their subtleness of colour made your eyes narrow.
Mixing a palette's within my means,
but my paintings are still more suited to a market-stall barrow.

But I painted well enough to exhibit, be commissioned and sell,
a palette of oils for canvas or board,
rich hues, deep tones, brush strokes, their story to tell.
For now, just like thin woodsmoke that's skyward soared
smaller watercolours ease my tired hands, yet inflame
      my heart well. ❧

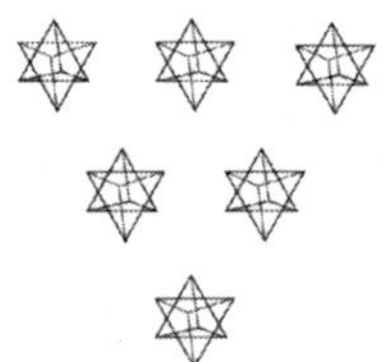

PLOT NIGHT

They poked underneath the pallets at the base,
and a disgruntled hedgepig ambled sleepily into the night:
"Better tired than roasted!"

Then the shout went up, in a guttural tone,
as the torch flared up into the night.
Suddenly the mound of broken wood, discarded furniture,
heaped and dried hedge
burst into flames,
sparks flying upward to puncture the sky.
The crowd stepped back as the bonfire took hold,
its' heat searing our faces,
its' smoke stinging our eyes.
Plot night had arrived.

Oh, the argument about whether there should be a Guy:
"It's only a bit of fun.....and the kiddies like it".
"Since when did we celebrate burning Catholics
          as a good thing?"
"it's not the same if we can't go around collecting
          —penny for the Guy"
"Since when did we believe that burning anyone for
          thinking differently was a good thing?"
The words had got harder since we first thought of them
          on a summer's night;
still, the fireworks are better on this dark November night.

Plot night had arrived,
with its' sparklers and toffee apples for the kids,
treacle toffee and ginger parkin to fend off hunger
until the foil-wrapped taters baked in the embers,
to then drip with butter
as we tossed them twixt burning hands.

We crushed the emptied beercans in our hands,
as the last rocket died in the sky
and weary children watched from bedroom windows.
Remember? Remember, fifth of November
        — gunpowder, treason and plot. ▨

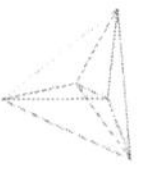
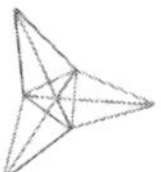
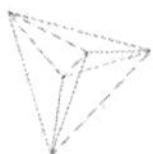
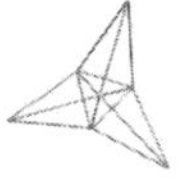

RAKU

When I was a potter
but arthritis stole my fingers:
raw clay, the pug-mill and strength
were the currency of my craft,
taking that clay to another plane.
Stoneware. Earthenware.
The poorly-done, leather-hard, broken-to-waste
so that only the best's fired, glazed and still lingers.

When I was a potter,
I used to mix my own glazes:
dull hues, full buckets of creamy sludge
applied to the biscuit-fired, coming alive
taking a night-kiln's heat to fire.
Stoneware. Earthenware.
The freshly-coated, hard-glazed, fresh from the pyre
clear, deep-coloured until its age crazes.

Then I was a potter,
using different techniques
making all manner of house-hold things.
Sometimes, dustbins full of sawdust, half-fired pots
set alight, creating a blazing heat.
Stoneware. Earthenware.
Plunged deep-glowing in the bucket at my feet,
cold water, steam, burnished pots, in my raku weeks. 

VOLCANO TREK

We had been warned:
"Wear layers, stout shoes and it's your own risk!".
We had flown in only two days before, yet this was
       the high point — literally.

Finally, the day dawned,
we trekked upwards into the smoke and the mist.
We picked our way, between red-hot rivulets on
       hard pumiced lava — carefully

Where the crater's edge formed,
we stood, roasting, looking into the abyss
at the seething, bubbling cauldron, as our feet
       shuffled backwards — prayerfully.

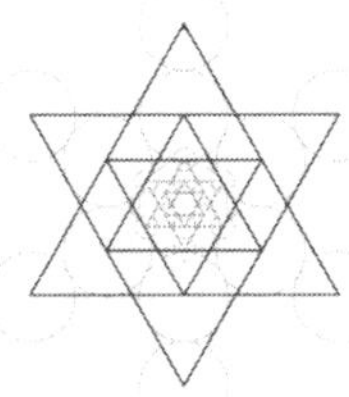

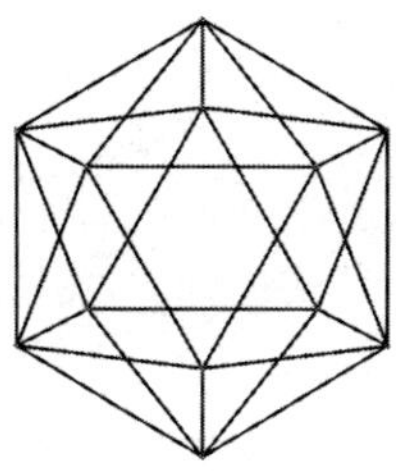

Water

BOOKSHOP AFLOAT...

There's a feisty, young woman called Sarah
whose joy is as a travelling bookseller,
once using the huge front basket of a tradesman's black bike
cycling all the way to the festival at Hay.
But she came into her own, when she met Joseph
a tidy but sixty-foot black barge or narrowboat, you see.
Filled with pamphlets and books, but nowhere for cooks,
she began to travel England, by river and cut, plying her trade,
sometimes trading her books for meals or a bath
       — what could be fairer?
Not much cash, not many sales, to make that bookseller grade
but her craft, the lady herself, Joseph, its stock, all had the looks,
to be the success that such thought and enterprise
         deserved to be.
Yet this internet age to such charms had made the people
         blind and deaf,
who would drop by for tea and cake from the towpath's way,
finding books to cherish but not at a price they would like.
So she'd moor up for the night, find a pasta supper,
        white wine from a cellar,
telling her tale, offering her books in exchange — now what
        could be fairer? ❧

NOTE: This poem is based upon a chance encounter with *The Books' Barge*. Its owner Sarah Henshaw tells her story in *The Bookshop that Floated Away* [London: Constable & Robinson, 2014]

CAEN HILL

Caen Hill rose before us, as some ghostly stairway
appearing through the morning's moist mist.
Its flight of twenty-nine locks, a testament to Rennie's vision,
the lie of land, the sweating of navvies and
      the passing of time.

The first eight, like an octave's scale, rehearsed away
as we worked through the repeating list.
The speed of our ascent, slowed by sloth and the
      downward boats' decision:
why fill each lock more than effort demands?
      "Waste water's a crime!".

The middle flight, with each pound calling us to stay,
to linger, take a walk, make a tryst.
The ducks, coots and voles scoot for scraps, a lone swan
      keeps guard by hissing:
here one loses track of the day's passing – not really a crime.

The last six – the rise to Devizes, high away,
a market town gem — not to be missed.
Nor a pint of local Wadsworth's 6-X, real ale beyond derision;
Journey's end? The Kennet and Avon beckons,
      asking for time.

COATE WATER

Winter, and the day is literally as cold as ice.
The lake is freezing at its edges,
as our fingers turn blue and our noses red.
The season's orb is golden orange in the sky of grey,
the divine painter is at work in the monochrome,
we hasten our pace, hardly breathing, making words unsaid.

Spring, and the greens are burgeoning in every shade,
the lake is rippling in its breadth,
as we walk and talk the familiar circling path.
The water looks like a dirty mirror losing its soul
as coupling swans and warring mallards claim
        each bankside knole
pausing as a man berates his dog's impulsive springtime bath.

Summer, and the sun is high, squinting the eyes.
The lake splashes with paddling youth
as parents shout caution and children ignore them.
The divers' high tower now abandoned to fate,
skeletally points at the sky — symbol of a bygone past,
when the lake and its park were still a day-trippers' gem.

Autumn has come with its golds, browns and orange,
the lake now still in its silver best
as the leaves turn into their rainbow shades of death
Now it is just you and I, the joggers and dog-walkers
making our circuits, sharing our hopes and watching for rain,
for this is the people's Coate, whatever season,
        colour or weather. ✌

CONISTON

The brooding nature of the hills around
are as nothing to the to the secrets and depths
reflected in Coniston Water.
Winds ruffle the surface to waves, without a sound,
the cold and the colour, betraying its depth
respected at Coniston Water.

The fells and the Old Man
act as witnesses to the water's doing
and man's undoing in Coniston Water.
A flash of light and Bluebird speed,
a rogue wave, and catapulting craft.
Donald's death – hard footage for Gina, his daughter.

Now more than the hills have to brood
as the world becomes a witness
for that recorded at Coniston Water.
Darkness had moved on the face of the deep
but now its shores seem to be asleep
as little is moving around Coniston Water. ✀

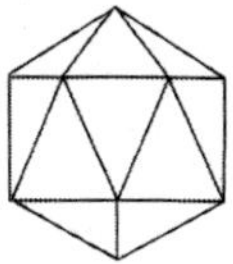

'Endless River'

"One learns more about a river from its estuary than its source",
wrote de Chardin. But there is knowledge in the intervening
          water's course.

What began with pot-head pixies, great-coated students
          and musicos,
sharing a saucerful of secrets and swirling light shows,
has meddled and matured through unboundaried echoes.

Like the child's innocence in the world's theatre of dreams,
our ears listen and minds wonder as they played out new scenes,
from Middle Earth to stadia grandeur, but held within
          vinyl's means,
we learned to expect more change than that theatre's dreams.

No longer small furry animals, great-coated in our hungry teams,
awaiting each new release , explaining truths oft beyond
          our means.

But they provided the soundtrack for a lifestyle and many rebels
          with a cause,
as successive waves of their creation resounded past the bores,
annotating lives through love and death, life and times,
          divorce and wars.

How much more than they were the piper at the gates of
          psychedelic dawn, who knows
but it was every atom-hearted mother's wish to witness
          success as it grows. ❧

Pigs might have flown as we wished we were there backstage
        at their shows,
we may have shunned our education but they never let us doze.

Who knows where that momentary lapse of reason goes?
As we lose ourselves in their wall of sound every time it flows...

Like the craziness of diamonds rolling in clear mountain streams,
their music rang more than division bells, and much more
        it seems
as their sound bent our minds like prisms pars up lightbeams.

That last album, *The Endless River* came after such
        significant pause
an estuary of arrival in which an untold world outpours.
Syd and Rick have already gone, lost to a dark side
        beyond science laws.
Yet although we might die, Pink Floyd still remain
        — an important tour de force. ✆

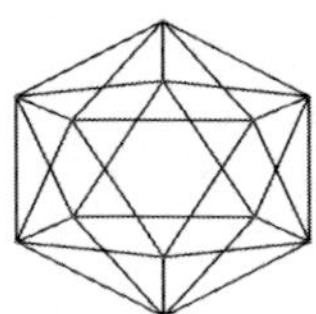

PORT LEITH

(*a poem for two voices*)

They chased the great leviathan from the sea to the land,
bleeding out for miles, to be gutted on the strand.
Just like Micah the prophet foretold,
the mountains stood as witnesses, black and white, all around
Port Leith.

For now the town lies rusting,
riddled with the cancer of asbestos,
still strangely drawing the eye
to the end of this bay of carnage.
Men were billeted here for months on end,
arriving with the callowness of youth
and the hungry greed of Scots deprivation,
to hone their killing and tone their muscling.

Far out in the southern ocean's cold,
it had begun as a struggle of titans,
brave oilskinned men with hand-held harpoons
pitted against the might of the whale.
Was it then fair or even just?
There only ever was to be one victor,
even if the hunt lasted for hours
the rewards were too great to fail.

For now the town lies rusting,
riddled with the cancer of what it once was:

a place of death, butchery and loss
of dignity for the hunter and humanity.
On locker doors, the topless girls flutter
now in the searing wind, coursing its ruin,
as once they fluttered their charms on screen,
in the cinema behind the workers' bar.

Far out in the barbarity of human minds,
they invented the explosive rocket harpoon,
mounted on fast boats — their quarry was doomed
to die, exhausted, drowning in its own blood.
Was it then fair or even just?
Now this was just a mechanised death,
the whales, older than their killers, hunted to a pause
then the harpoon lanced, exploding its guts.

For then the town was bustling,
riddled with answers to questions unsaid:
the tugs towed the whales to the bay,
the winches dragging them onto that bloody strand.
The flensers knew their trade well, holding
their blades so the winches peeled back the skin,
before the cutters carved and oil was drained
into large drums as tall as three men.

When the whalers first came, the whales were there:
so many — blue, humpbacked, southern rights and minkes, too.
Even orcas would follow the first factory ships,
knowing that guts and the spoils made an easy meal.
Was it then fair or even just?

Salvesons took more than their pound of flesh,
buying off the Scots and Edinburgh public
with high wages and some more penguins for the zoo.

The end came, the shanty town busting,
riddled with questions, the answers unsaid:
the whales had gone – not enough left in the sea,
Gone was the profit, so great the inhumanity.
Port Leith was abandoned, its killers went home,
as did the men who had worked with bloody hands,
leaving the strand and the winch to seals and the birds,
iron sheds left to rust as winters did their worst.

Far out in the southern ocean's cold,
there are some who have returned to kill
loading their once-sentient prey onto factory ships,
dodging the truly brave protestors' boats.
What was unfair is still unjust!
That South Georgian bay is now abandoned
to the black witnessing mountains around Port Leith,
streaked with the white falls of glacial snow.

They have chased the great leviathan from the seas,
to bleed out for miles, once gutted on the strand.
Just like Micah the prophet foretold,
the mountains stood as witnesses, black and white, all around
the now silent Port Leith. ❧

REFLECTIONS

Cool, clear water on an unruffled day,
seemed to be the mark of this unhurried summer
as we sojourned from valley to valley.
The dog-eared Wainwright never far from the hand,
should we try this climb or ridge today?
Or should we pause on the lakeside as if waiting for Galilee?

Mirror, mirror, on the dark hallway wall
seems to declare ghosts of the cottage's former guests,
as we sojourn from fortnight to summer.
The large, ticking clock never silent at night,
keeps me awake and children in thrall.
Or should we not reflect and begrudge the passing of time?

To reflect and reflect on the passage of time
tells of a childhood, lost in the Lakeland of summers ago,
as we went there for longer each year.
The familiar large house, hallway and views,
occupying this place, in rain or in shine.
But knowing my day would come when I would choose...

Cool, clear water in an unmarked Greek bay
proved to be the spark of that backpacking escape
as we ferried from island to island.
The long-feared Baedeker telling us 'move on'
rather than pause, bathe in the heat of the day.
Or sleep beneath the lemon trees
        necklacing the deserted beach?

Mirror, mirror, behind the bottled shelves
keeping account of the emptying spirits,
as we move tastes from bottle to bottle
This Cretan bar's tab gets longer with each night
as we forget budgets to indulge ourselves.
Or is it to recall "Do you remember that night in Ag Nick?"

To reflect and reflect on the passage of time
tells of mis-spent years, backpacking Greek islands, aeons away,
as we moved from friend to partner to wife.
The familiar ferries, mountains and ports,
occupied rich slow days, in blazing sunshine.
But knowing the day would come when we would choose...

Cool, clear water in our gite's stone-lined pool
as we dived down, exploring its dark depths
as we tarry from day to lazy day.
The too-near neighbour accepting the shouted "Hi"
to invade our peace, jump in our silver's cool.
Or should we have said something more,
          ring-fencing our private place?

Mirror, mirror, above the smoke-blacked log stove
watching us let go of our middle-aged British reserve,
as we discard our clothes in summer's heat.
The kitchen's calendar has marked off the weeks
for new names, new folks, a French life to behove.
Or should we have booked to stay for the season...?

To reflect and reflect on the passage of time
tells of our children, trapped Dordogne orphans
       just as we weren't,
but we were once captive to the Cumbrian class.
The familiar night-boat, journey and francs,
occupied their minds, each summertime.
But knowing new days would come when we could choose…

Cool, clear water beyond the but-and-ben's front door,
as we drive through the night to our Scottish retreat,
with its white walls reflected all-year in that lochside.
We have a ticking clock, books and a warm bed,
below a mirror, next to the log-stove's chimney.
Life's questions mainly answered
      — we just reflect together instead. ❧

SALTMARSH

The ghost of the child Grenfell paddles across the Dee.
The canvas skin, the cane skeleton's no protection from the cold
of the rushing current of the tidal salt,
grounding on the sunken marram tufts, shallow then deep.
Startled birds rise to the headwind, nature's compass to behold,
proving courage, risking death – a young man's fault.

The punt of the hunter Scott glides past the old lighthouse.
Lying flat, silent, the huge punt gun points up at the ready,
waiting, waiting, for the flock to take flight.
Warming the heart with thoughts of food,
     back at the bright house,
one moment, a flicker, wing-beats, hold the gun steady.
Boom! Then boom! The dead fall as day turns night.

The ghost of the naturalist Scott strides the saltmarsh,
from the Berkeley canal, past the Swan Pond to the tidal reed.
Slimbridge sits as the exemplar wetland,
calling summer's migrants then geese in January's harsh
weather and snowstorm. Students and birders watch,
     learn and heed
as man and nature, as one can stand. ৯

SEVERN CROSSING

The Aust ferry of childhood years has gone,
replaced by the now old bridge to Chepstow
and that cable-stayed bridge, second-to-none,
motorway routes to Wales, life-on-the-go.
And yet I am always left wondering
how Westminster dares to collect the tolls
on Welsh soil, like some Tudor princeling?
The bridge is paid for, why steal from the Welsh?
For me, these roads are gateways to hill and coast
in the proud land where the red dragon roars,
the people share that pride in their talk and boast:
a nation now reborn as tour de force.
But our journey is now caught on the tide
moving downstream, the Bristol channel to ride. ✺

NOTE: This poem forms part of a seven-sonnet cycle about
the River Severn, which will be published in its entirety in a future
publication

SNOWFLAKE

In finest filigree,
the ice had laced its hexagon.
Unique in form — silent in the air,
blown and tossed by the winter wind.

Yet together, they made a flurry
of flakes to bleach the land and darken the air,
making monochrome of the brown earth
and winter-bared trees.
Spun together like candy-floss at a fair,
the flurries whipped up into a blanket
carpeting the ground and disguising the lake.
Woven together, by the winds of winter,
they made cotton-wool of the sky
to its farthest horizon.

In that white filigree,
their patterns shone against my dark sleeve,
as its warmth stole their soul,
draining their very life away to nothing. ❧

TALES OF A RIVERBANK

As children, we were told
"This was the river at the end of the world",
for the wildwood lay beyond.
It was the furthest part of our triangular Sunday walk,
as we blackberried along where the river curled,
helping us to see that to nature we belonged.

Then the bad news arrived,
"There's been a spillage upstream at the old works"
dead minnows were the first sign.
Then the oil- slicked current began to weave its rainbow surface
of death, telling of responsibilities shirked,
as no-one was prosecuted for such a crime.

For years, the experts said,
"No swimming, drinking or eating bankside plants",
as the river turned black and dead.
The old works closed and the rivermen
        cleared the banks and algaic weeds,
Fall and Spring alike, amidst others cant,
as more and more voices rang untrue in my head.

Now I tell my children,
"Look at the heron, it nests at the upstream weir,
catching the returning fish and the young frogs".
For now we go blackberrying on our Sunday morning walks,
looking for those fish in water gin-clear,
not having to worry about the splashing of our dogs.

Some years more, our guide speaks
"We might see them but we need to be there at dawn".
Silently we go, smelling spraint on the bank.
First, the strong head of a dog otter ploughs
        across the wide stream,
then we hear the cry of the cubs, last spring born,
before their mother with a fish, swims to the far bank. ❧

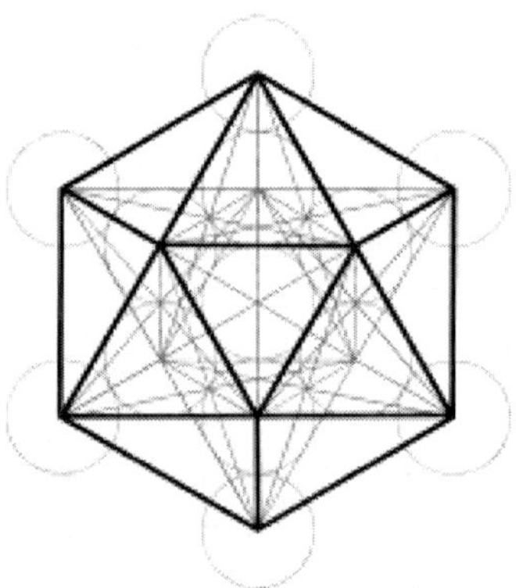

"THE RAIN IT RAINETH EVERY DAY"

The train pulled into Penzance,
reeling in the track from Marazion,
like the fisherman reels in the tired trout.
It was our monthly pilgrimage
to the old family home, shuttered and warm.
We walked from the station, bags in hand,
unlocking the door, uncorking the wine – time out!

We had woken almost late -
you slept on, as I slipped from the warmth
for that day's *Times*, hot rolls and a first glance.
The gallery was still empty,
as I bounded stairs, familiarly worn.
entering the room, I crossed to the bench
just a few minutes, Garstin at his best to glance.

I waited patiently
for your return from your favourite shops,
with bags of remnant cloth, thread, bread and emptied purse.
Had Norman had to wait so long to paint,
having seen the everyday, dawn to dusk to dawn.
but he who can catch the mirrored promenade
the still-standing tower, the rain's beauty, lifting its curse?

I sipped at my coffee
on the café terrace of Penlee House
we had seen the painting together again
          and you gazed at the trees.
I reflected upon Shakespeare's muse,
scratching away with his goose quill, ink-stained and worn
bringing that *Twelfth Night* into life and onto stage
boyhood memories, constant rain and couplets that tease.

Sunday dawned wet and cold,
we hunkered down – re-thought the day:
a pub lunch for two, then a walk by the sea.
The spume whipped across as in Garstin's painting,
gulls gliding on winds and now upward borne,
taking our breath, salt-spray drenching our feet:
turning inland, we made our way back to Penlee. ❧

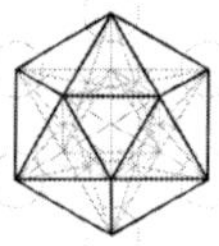

NOTE: This poem is written in celebration of my favourite English painting 'The rain it raineth every day', by Norman Garstin (1847-1926). He was a member of the Newlyn School and this work is now permanently housed in the Gallery at Penlee House, Penzance. Garstin named it after a line from Shakespeare's *Twelfth Night*.

THE WEIR POOL

The weir pool was a secret haunt of my youth,
it was hidden away at the end of a lane
by a hermit's woodland hut with its turf roof.
He taught us to tickle trout and other skills for life's gain –
cooking sausages on twigs, spuds in ashes, in sun and rain,
whilst sharing ideas in our stumbling for truth.

Our parents warned us against that old weir pool,
where Ned the tramp, had been found, drowned ,
     some years before;
then the papers wrote him off as a drunken fool.
The hermit protested with letters and outside the court.
Ned's death and the hermit taught us to know
     what we stand for —
to live as we believe, not by some others' rules.

They said the weir pool represented danger:
a place to cast your line and yet a place to meet
but who? Not just friends or someone much stranger,
half-hidden in the trees, giving shade from the summer's heat.
Yet we all survived, learned to fish, live wild to nature's beat
until they fenced the weir, now patrolled by rangers. ❧

ONCE I WAS...

Once I was a potter,
until arthritis stole my hands:
stealing the ability to throw cold clay for a winter's morning.
Selling my labour to buy clay cut from a neighbour's land.
Making vases or a set of mugs with or without the coffeepot
was all grist to my potting days' mill.
My wheel and kiln are gone but still
it hurts as the loss of my craft is dawning.

Once I was a singer
until heart disease stole my breath
taking floor singing from me and opportunities to play a set.
The guitars still hang upon my wall, flute upon a shelf.
Making music or jamming with friends, for the jazz or
        folk club nights,
was just part of my everyday life.
Voice and song gone, leaves pain like a knife,
twisting that "no return" and never "not yet".

Once I was a painter,
until age robbed my energies
for bold big canvases in favour of tiny watercolours.
The studio echoes as each canvas is gradually sold.
For now the translucence of water enlivens those landscapes
auto-suggesting to the mind's eye,
an untaken journey, touching the sky.
Changing perspectives for other escapes.

Once I was a writer
with just a mind full of ideas…
but now I am a writer with discipline to write more each day.
It is a craft never finally learned, full of hopes and fears.
Tacked above my desk, Heaney's words speak to wield the pen
        like a spade,
turning the words like turning the earth,
revising – refining – full page – new birth,
each article, chapter, verse in its own way.

Once I was full of life,
'sound in wind and limb', like a fit horse,
but now my heart is failing however sound in mind and soul
        I am.
Once I could dig clay from the earth and barrow it home
        to weather.
Once I had breath to carouse with a band, rehearsing
        the night away.
All that is left is the passion
burning like fire, life's final ration,
until heartbeat and breath, ebb like water away.

Once I was. ℘

FIRST LINES

END PIECE

For those of us who were students or even teenagers at the height of the progressive rock era, the themes of this anthology are no surprise. I was fascinated by the musical fusion of the Third Ear Band, which drew upon English medieval and folk music, Indian raga and other sources. Their first 1969 album *Alchemy* was cleverly titled and was soon followed in 1970 by *Air, Earth, Fire and Water*. The philosophy of the interplay of the elements was often returned to in Incredible String Band songs and the 1972 album, *The Alchemist*, by the rock band, Home. The rock band, Free's album *Fire and Water* was another in the soundtrack of my life.

Soon I found myself writing college essays upon the role of alchemy and its relation to institutional religion, in the late medieval period of Britain and Europe. The works of Roger Bacon (1214-94) and George Ripley (1415-90) found their own space on my bookshelves. The embryonic versions of several of these poems date back to this period in my life.

Only two of these poems are appearing in exactly the form that they have been previously been published – you will have to guess which two. Eleven of these poems have appeared singly in other regional anthologies or chapbooks. Over the last three decades, nine more have been published in a variety of local poetry magazines — three Cornish poems together in a now-defunct Penwith-based journal, whose name I forget (sorry). But, apart from those first-mentioned two, whether it is a singular word or line, the addition or subtraction of a 'verse' or couplet, or a change in punctuation, they have all undergone some further and final revision for this volume.

But it was meeting Rowan, a pagan acquaintance 'at the stones' shortly after the publication of my 2011 collection, *Avebury: Rime & Time*, that prompted this collection, with his question "What's next – earth, air, fire and water?". Back home, whilst playing Home, the ISBs and the Third Ear Band, I reviewed the old year-on-year exercise books (full of my poetry and prose), now computer USBs, and realised that I already had the beginnings of many Earth Air Fire Water poems. So on we went... and now we are here, with this volume in your hands.

Andrew Francis
Winter solstice 2014

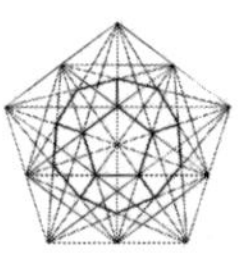

Andrew Francis is a poet, author and community theologian. He lives in north Wiltshire.

Previously he has exhibited his hand-thrown pottery, sold his own paintings and played in various occasional folk-groups. He enjoys cooking for friends, baking bread, making hedgerow wines, jams and chutneys as well as vegetable growing as a keen allotmenteer. He is a member of the Poetry Society and the Cat Survival Trust, which helps coordinate the breeding of snow-leopards and other wild feline species. He is also a life member of Friends of Swindon Art Gallery, which holds the best UK collection of twentieth-century watercolours.

In some extensive notes for a future autobiographical piece, he has written: 'Enjoying good things in life was always part of my dream. In travelling to many countries, enjoying the local culture and their regional cuisine, I learned much. I would rarely return home to Britain without a local recipe book or a desire to learn more about the art and history of where I had just been...'.

'I suppose that living in France, studying in the US, being seconded to different agencies (like the BBC or the UK's Anabaptist Network) and short work assignments in Europe change your perspectives. It means that when you get back home, you enjoy simply living (and living simply), sharing bread and other food with family and friends...'

Following undergraduate studies in law and theology, he went onto to gain an MTh for his work on radical theological movements, and then a doctorate in Princeton, USA for work about how Christian communities use and share food. He says "when life quietens down", he hopes to complete his unfinished MA in History of Art and an MSc in Zoology.

His theological writings include *Anabaptism: Radical Christianity* (Antioch Press, 2010), *Hospitality and Community After Christendom* (Paternoster, 2012) and the much anticipated *Shalom: The Jesus Manifesto* (Paternoster, 2016). His work on Christian social policy includes *What in God's Name are You Eating* (Cascade, 2014) about food ethics and he is co-editor (with Trisha Dale) of *Foxes Have Holes...* (Ekklesia, 2016), a book on UK housing policy. He has also written a biographical study of the political theologian D*orothee Soelle: Life and Work* (Imagier, 2014). He has a previous volume of poetry, *Avebury: Rime and Time* (Kettle Press, 2010). He has written book introductions, hymns, several academic and journal articles.

He is currently revising a work on global economics and ethics, entitled *OIKOS: God's Big Word for a Small Planet* scheduled for 2017 publication (Cascade, USA) as well as preparing a further volume of poetry for Kettle Press. He continues to be a popular conference speaker, church preacher and performance poet.

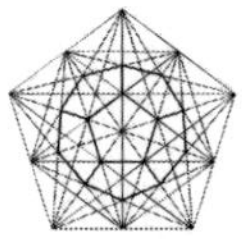